READING COMPREHENSION

Written by **Shannon Keeley**

Illustrated by **David Coulson**

FlashKids™

This book belongs to

_____

ISBN-13: 978-1-4114-9921-8
ISBN-10: 1-4114-9921-2

For more information, please visit _www.flashkidsbooks.com_
Please submit changes or report errors to _www.flashkidsbooks.com/errors_

Printed and bound in China

Spark Publishing
120 Fifth Avenue
New York, NY 10011

Dear Parent,

Once young children have learned to read, the next important step is to ensure that they understand and retain the information they encounter. The passages and activities contained in this book will provide your child with plenty of opportunities to develop these vital reading comprehension skills. The more your child reads and responds to literature, the greater the improvement you will see in his or her mastery of reading comprehension. To get the most from *Reading Comprehension*, follow these simple steps:

- Provide a comfortable and quiet place for your child to work.
- Encourage your child to work at his or her own pace.
- Help your child with the problems if he or she needs it.
- Offer lots of praise and support.
- Encourage your child to work independently to gain confidence in his or her problem solving skills.
- Allow your child to enjoy the fun actvities in this book.
- Most of all, remember that learning should be fun!

Visit us at *www.flashkidsbooks.com* for free downloads, informative articles, and valuable parent resources!

Phillis Wheatley

In the late 1700s, most slaves were allowed to read or write. During this ti there was one black slave who not only wr poems, but published them too! Her na was Phillis Wheatley, and she was the African-American poet.

Phillis was born in Senegal, Africa. At age of seven she was kidnapped by sl traders. A ship brought her to Boston, wh John and Susannah Wheatley purcha her. The Wheatleys treated Phillis more lik member of the family than a slave. They saw Phillis writing on the wall with chalk day, but they didn't punish her. Instead, they helped her learn to read and write. By time Phillis was twelve, she could read Greek, Latin, and verses from the Bible.

Phillis started writing poetry when she was only thirteen years old. Her first po was published in 1767 in the *Newport Mercury* newspaper. When a preacher in Bos died in 1770, Phillis wrote a poem about him. Many people in Boston liked her po and Phillis became well-known. A few years later, a book with 39 of Phillis's poems v published in London. It was the first book published by an African-American.

In 1776, Phillis wrote a poem to George Washington and mailed it to him. Washing thought Phillis was very talented, and he invited her to meet him. When the Wheatl passed away, Phillis became a free woman. She used her talent with words to write antislavery letter, which she also sent to George Washington.

Phillis married a free black man in 1778, and she moved away from Boston. She wr more poems, but her fame declined. She had an unhappy marriage and eventu moved back to Boston, where she passed away. After her death, people continued publish her poems and letters. Today people still study and read her writings.

Find your way through the maze by connecting the events in the correct sequence.

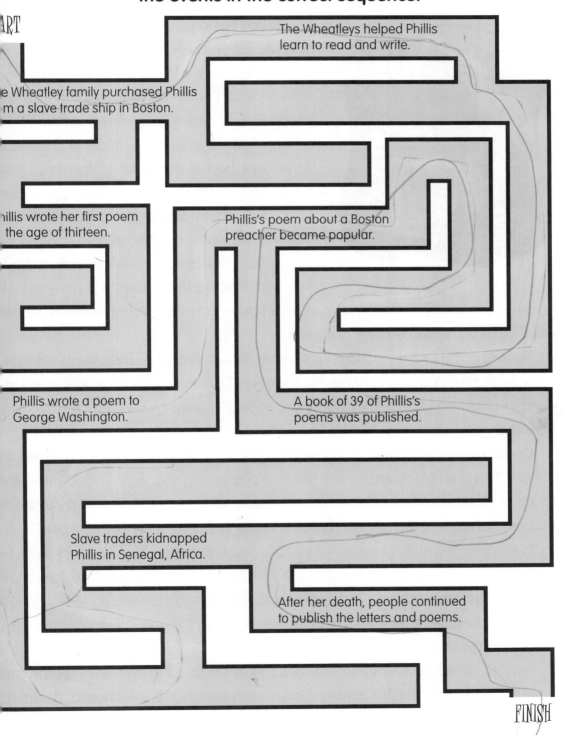

START

The Wheatleys helped Phillis learn to read and write.

The Wheatley family purchased Phillis from a slave trade ship in Boston.

Phillis wrote her first poem at the age of thirteen.

Phillis's poem about a Boston preacher became popular.

Phillis wrote a poem to George Washington.

A book of 39 of Phillis's poems was published.

Slave traders kidnapped Phillis in Senegal, Africa.

After her death, people continued to publish the letters and poems.

FINISH

What Color Is Your Crayon?

Do you like to color? The average American spends about three hours a week coloring w crayons. That's over 150 hours a year! In fact, by time a person turns ten years old, he or she probably worn down about 730 crayons.

The first crayons were made in Europe, Americans had to pay a lot of money to imp them. Two men named Edwin Binney and Har Smith wanted to find a cheaper way to m crayons. They had already created a wax cra for marking crates and boxes in their factory. they had chemists develop a similar crayon for to use. Edwin Binney's wife came up with the name "Crayola," which combines the Fre word for chalk, "craie," with the word for oil.

The first box of Crayola crayons was sold in 1903 for five cents. The original colors w black, blue, brown, green, orange, red, violet, and yellow. In 1949, Crayola increased number of crayons to 48. They added more shades with names like apricot, salm periwinkle, and cornflower.

One of the colors added in 1949 was "Prussian Blue." The color was named a "Prussia," an area of Eastern Europe. As time passed, Prussia was divided into differ countries. Teachers wrote letters to Crayola because the word "Prussian" confused th students. As a result, Crayola changed the name of that color to "midnight blue."

In 1958, the number of colors rose to 64, and among the 16 new colors were n blue, goldenrod, and lavender. Crayola introduced eight fluorescent colors in 19 which brought the total up to 72. Eight more fluorescent colors were added in 1990. meant that there were 80 colors at this time, including the new fluorescent shades radical red and magic mint.

Crayola introduced sixteen new colors in 1993, and this time they let the pu come up with ideas for the names. Colors such as macaroni & cheese, denim, amrock were added to bring the total number of colors up to 96. In 1998, that number mped from 96 to 120 with shades including cotton candy and outer space.

Crayola started out with a small x of eight crayons, and now both the mpany and the crayon boxes are ch bigger. Every year they produce ut three million crayons. They now l their crayons in 80 different countries d twelve languages!

Use the information from the passage to complete the graph below. Make a point on the graph to show the total number of colors Crayola made each year. Then connect the points.

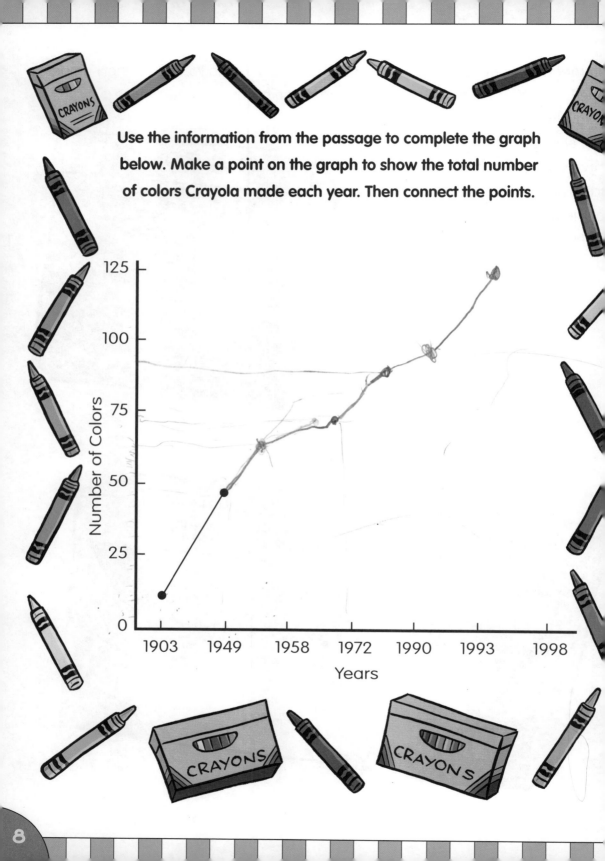

Number of Colors

125
100
75
50
25
0

1903   1949   1958   1972   1990   1993   1998

Years

> A <u>conclusion</u> is something not stated in the passage. You draw conclusions using clues from the text and your own logic.

1. Circle the most logical conclusion you can draw from the passage.
   - (a) Crayola crayons were popular and sold well. People liked having lots of color choices and wanted more new colors.
   - b) Nobody was buying Crayola crayons because they were too messy.
   - c) The crayons were too expensive because there were so many colors. Crayola will never add any more new colors.

2. Read the conclusion and circle the clues that support it.
   There may be more than one correct clue!

   Conclusion: Crayola listens to what the public thinks about their crayons.

   Clues:
   - a) Since their company started, Crayola has made 100 billion crayons.
   - b) When teachers wrote letters to Crayola, they changed a color name from "Prussian blue" to "midnight blue."
   - c) The eight original colors were yellow, red, orange, green, blue, violet, brown, and black.
   - d) In 1993, Crayola asked the public to help name sixteen new crayon colors.

3. Find clues from the reading passage that support the conclusion.
   List the facts on the lines below.

   Conclusion: Coloring is a popular activity that lots of kids enjoy.

   Clues: ① there are sow meany choses to chose from
   ②. they are fun to drow piccherers with
   ③. they are not thal espenive they are very chep,

9

Catching the Fog

For most of us, fog is a type of weather. But for some people, fog is a source of water! In places where there isn't enough fresh water, people can collect the fog and turn it into water. How does all this work?

If you've ever walked through a patch of fog, you might have noticed that your skin and hair felt damp. This is because fog is actually made of tiny water droplets. Scientists are helping people collect these droplets to make drinking water. Often, these people live in towns where there is no fresh water source. They rely on trucks to deliver fr water, which is expensive. It's better for a town to be able to make its own fresh water.

People have always looked to rain as a source of fresh water. Since rain falls tow the ground, it can easily be collected into tanks. But the water droplets that make up don't hit the ground. Instead, they float in the air. Fog is a lot like a cloud that hovers c to the ground. To turn fog into water, you have to catch the water droplets.

A fog catcher is made of nets stretched between two posts. Usually the nets are up on a hilltop or in a valley where fog often settles. As fog drifts by, the nets trap water droplets. Beads of water run down the nets and collect into gutters. The gut and pipes guide the water into large tanks where it can be stored. A fog catcher collect up to 10,000 liters of water a day. Scientists have helped set up fog catchers towns in Chile, Nepal, and Mexico.

Fog catchers are a great way for people in isolated towns to have their own fr water source. Centuries before scientists created fog-catching nets, nature was mak fog into water on its own. As fog passed through the mountains, large leaves trapp the droplets just like the nets do. Native people learned to drink the tiny pools of wo that collected on the leaves. Thanks to modern fog catchers, enough water can be mo to supply a whole town!

Read each sentence and check whether it gives the main idea of the passage or a supporting detail.

	Main Idea	Supporting Detail
Fog is a lot like a cloud that hovers close to the ground.		✓
A fog catcher can collect up to 10,000 liters of water a day.		✓
Fog catchers are a great way for people in isolated towns to have their own fresh water source.	✓	
A fog catcher is made of nets stretched between two posts.	✓	
Scientists have helped set up fog catchers for towns in Chile, Nepal, and Mexico.	✓	
Native people learned to drink the tiny pools of water that collected on the leaves.		✓
In places where there isn't enough fresh water, people can collect the fog and turn it into water.	✓	
Thanks to modern fog catchers, enough water can be made to supply a whole town!		✓

Puppy Raising

Gabe had been begging his father for a dog for months. But when his dad ca[me] home one day with a Golden Retriever puppy, Gabe was in for a big surprise.

"This is Tracer, and he's a very special dog," Gabe's dad explained. "We're going [to] help raise this puppy to become a guide dog."

"You mean the kind of dog that helps blind people?" Gabe asked.

"Exactly," said his dad. "Before Tracer can be a guide dog, he needs to develop soc[ial] skills. He'll live with us for many months, and then he'll go back to the training sch[ool]. They will match him with a blind person to be his owner."

"This is the worst idea ever!" Gabe shouted. "I don't want a dog I'll just have to g[ive] away!" Gabe stormed off to his room.

At first, Gabe avoided Tracer. Tracer wore a special vest that explained he was a de dog in training. When Tracer was working, people were not supposed to pet him lay with him. But Tracer also had time to play, and Gabe couldn't resist playing with . When Tracer got to be bigger, he went to shops and restaurants with Gabe and his d. They taught him to be confident and friendly, but not to seek attention. Gabe and dad also taught Tracer voice commands like "sit" and "stay." Gabe enjoyed watching cer learn so much.

Months passed, and it was time for Tracer to go back to the school. When Gabe had ay goodbye to Tracer, he felt angry again. It seemed so unfair.

Tracer finished his training at the school, and he was leaving to live with a blind son. Gabe and his dad were invited to the school to meet Tracer's new owner. As they ve to the school Gabe was upset that Tracer was going to live with someone else. er all, they had raised him!

As soon as Gabe saw Tracer with his new owner, his feelings changed. He was ud to see Tracer dressed in a new guide vest, ready for his new owner.

"Thank you for giving Tracer such a good home," the owner said. "In helping to raise cer, you've helped me as well."

Gabe was sad to say goodbye to Tracer, but he wasn't angry anymore. He knew that cer was going to a good home where he was needed. The owner even told Gabe that could visit Tracer whenever he wanted.

On the drive home, Gabe was the one who had a surprise for his dad.

"I think we should raise another puppy to become a guide dog!" Gabe said.

Decide if the sentence describes the story's setting, conflict, resolution, or theme. Connect each sentence with the correct word.

1. Gabe meets Tracer's new owner and realizes he is going to a good home.

2. The story takes place at Gabe's home and at the dog training school.

3. Gabe is upset that they will have to give Tracer away after helping train him.

4. Giving away something you love is hard, but helping others makes the sacrifice worth it.

Setting

Conflict

Resolution

Theme

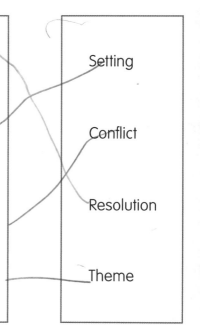

Summarize the plot of the story.

The plot of the story is that tracer got to go to a new home aater his traing is done.

Answer the questions.

Why did Gabe storm off to his room when his dad first brought Tracer home?

he could not cape him for ever.

What did Gabe and his dad teach Tracer?

Some tricks like sat ant stay.

How did Gabe feel on the way to the dog school?

he felt sad becase tracer was going to have a new onere

How did Gabe feel after meeting Tracer's new owner?

he fclt thertracer heed to go whith him,

What did Tracer's owner tell Gabe when they met?

that he cad came ano vist when ever he wants.

Why did Gabe's feelings change at the end of the story?

he fclt sad and poud becuse he did someing good

Why do you think Gabe's dad wanted them to be puppy trainers?

for gabe to get a dog

Would you want to be a puppy trainer? What are the good things and bad things?

I would hot want to be one becuse I eant cape the doo,

15

The Hot Dog and the Bun

As you read the passage, look for the underlined sentences. If the statement is fact, write an F in the box. If it's an opinion, write an O.

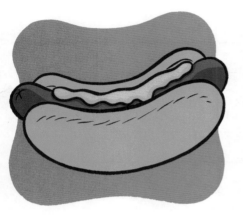

1. [O] <u>On a warm summer day, there's noth better than firing up the grill and cooking some to hot dogs.</u> In fact, each summer Americans eat ab 7 billion hot dogs. Many of these hot dogs are ed at summer baseball games. 2. [F] <u>During e baseball season, fans eat about 26 million hot do</u> Babe Ruth once ate so many hot dogs at a base game he had to go to the hospital! 3. [O] <u>The l time to have a hot dog is during the month of J which is National Hot Dog Month.</u>

Americans tend to eat more hot dogs in the summer, but hot dogs are actually popular year-round. Their popularity has made them an American symbol. 4. [F] <u>When King George VI visited the United States from England, he asked to try an American food.</u> So President Roosevelt served him a hot dog. 5. [ ] <u>After all, nothing is more American than a hot dog!</u> Or is it?

The idea for the hot dog actually started in Germany, where sausage was popular. 6. [F] <u>In German, sausage is called a *dachshund,* which means "little d</u> When Germans moved to the United States, they brou their "little dogs" with them. Some say that Germans hot sausages inside milk buns and sold them from ca in New York City. Other people say that the idea for bun started somewhere else.

The idea for the bun might have come from a man named Charles Feltman. 7.☐ Feltman started out selling pies from his pie cart to Coney Island bars. He came up with the idea of selling sausages on warm rolls, since he could easily prepare them in his cart. 8.☐ Feltman's "Coney Island Hot Dogs" became very popular and he opened his own restaurants.

Other people say the bun idea came from a man named Anton Feuchtwanger. According to the story, Anton was selling hot sausages at a big fair in St. Louis. The sausages were too hot to hold, so Anton ned people white gloves. When nobody returned the gloves, on asked his brother-in-law for help. He was a baker, and he me up with the idea for long rolls to hold the hot meat. 9.☐ s is an unlikely story, so it's probably not true.

Did the idea for the bun come from Germans, Charles man, or Anton Feuchtwanger? Nobody knows for sure. ☐ We do know that Americans eat lots of hot dogs—the erage American eats 60 a year!

Sleeping Feet

Ouch! Your foot tingles and it feels like you're walk on pins and needles. Somebody tells you that your foot "fallen asleep." How can your foot be asleep while yo still awake? What causes that tingling feeling?

It all starts with your body's nervous system. Th are millions of tiny nerves throughout your body. Imag a highway filled with cars driving in a loop. Signals fr your nerves are like cars: they travel up to the brair give a message, then they return to the body part v a message from the brain. If a large tree suddenly across the highway, what would happen? The cars would be blocked! They couldn't up to the brain or back to the body parts.

This is what happens when your foot "falls asleep." When you sit on your foo sleep on your arm, you put pressure on your body part. Too much pressure is like tree in the road. It blocks the pathway from the body part to the brain. The nerves c send their messages to the brain.

What happens when a tree blocks a road? A siren rings in the distance, warn drivers that there is danger. A truck races to the spot, removes the tree, and the cars flow again. When communication between nerves and the brain stops, your body ser out an alarm too. The tingling you feel in your body part is that alarm. It's telling you change your body position and lift the pressure off the body part that tingles.

Listening to your body's alarm is important. If you let that pathway remain blocked several hours, it can cause permanent damage to your nerves. The tingling is your boc way of warning you. Because it hurts, it prompts you to change your body position.

As you start to move around, it feels like you're walking on pins and needles. T feeling is your nerves "waking up" and starting to flow. With time the nerves returr normal, and the tingling slowly fades. Pretty soon, your nerves are back on the ro and the highway to your brain is buzzing with new messages.

d your way through the maze by connecting the events in the correct sequence.

START

You sit on your foot and place too much pressure on it.

The tingling fades and your nerves return to normal.

The pressure blocks the pathway from your foot to your brain.

You fall asleep on your arm and put too much pressure on it.

Nerves cannot send or receive messages from the brain.

The nerves slowly "wake up" and start to flow again.

Your nerves suffer permanent damage.

Your foot starts to tingle, so you change positions.

FINISH

Wagons Going West

Traveling across the country today is fast and easy. Airplanes, cars, and trains co[...] people to their destinations in hours or days. But back in the 1800s, traveling acr[...] the country took four to six months. Ranchers, farmers, miners, and traders trave[...] westward to make new lives for themselves in unsettled land. These pioneers walk[...] ten to fifteen miles a day, over hills, mountains, and prairies. It was a long, hard journ[...] but they had wagons to help them make the trip.

The Conestoga was a type of wagon used on many of these journeys. There were ee main parts to the wagon: the wagon box, the cover, and the undercarriage. The gon box was like a long boat. The floor sloped in the middle, which kept barrels m falling out if the wagon went uphill or downhill. The side boards slanted outward help keep water out.

The wagon cover was called the "bonnet." The bonnet protected the wagon's tents from rain and wind. The bonnet was held up by large wooden bows. Planks vood were soaked in water until they became bendable. Then they were bent into a hape and allowed to dry. The bonnet was stretched over the wooden bows, making oof for the wagon.

The undercarriage included the wheels and running gear. There were four round tires with a hub in the middle of each one. A long piece of wood called a "tongue" etched out from the front of the wagon. At the end of the tongue was a handle called yoke." Pushing forward on the yoke moved the wagon forward. Powerful teams of en or mules hauled the heavy loads.

The Conestoga was favored by traders along the Santa Fe Trail, a famous route m Missouri to New Mexico. They liked using the Conestoga because it was large d durable. It could haul up to six tons. Settlers traveling all the way to Oregon and ifornia tried the Conestoga, but it was too big and heavy. Even the strongest oxen ıld not complete the journey pulling a Conestoga. So, a smaller wagon called a irie schooner was made. It had the same design as the Conestoga, but was half size. Families filled the prairie schooners with their food and belongings, and then lked alongside.

Whether by Conestoga or prairie schooner, people relied on their wagons to travel st. Wagons helped shape history as they made it possible for people to make this rney.

Use the information from the passage to complete the diagram below. Label the parts of the wagon using the words in the word box.

wagon box	tire	bow
hub	tongue	yoke
	bonnet	

Bow

wagon
box but

hub
tire

togue
yoke

1. Circle the most logical conclusion you can draw from the passage.

   a) The Conestoga wagon was better than the prairie schooner because it was bigger.

   b) It took too long for the wagons to travel long distances, so people should have waited until the train was invented.

   c) In the 1800s, wagons were well-designed marvels that made western travel possible.

2. Read the conclusion and circle the clues that support it. There may be more than one correct clue!

   Conclusion: The trail to Oregon and California was longer and more difficult than the Santa Fe trail.

   Clues:

   a) Oxen could not complete the journey to Oregon pulling a Conestoga wagon.

   b) Wood was soaked in water until it was bendable, then made into bows.

   c) In Santa Fe, Mexicans traded goods with people from Missouri.

   d) People needed smaller wagons called "prairie schooners" to travel to California and Oregon.

3. Find clues from the reading passage that support the conclusion. List the facts on the lines below.

   Conclusion: The design of the wagon helped settlers overcome obstacles on the trail.

   Clues: 1. it is easy

   2. it make you faster

   3. you can carry save

   4. you don't get tired

The Hero's Journey

When we say the word "hero," we are usually talking about someone we admire. [We] might look up to a hero because he or she did something brave or important. We also co[me] across heroes in the stories we read. Often, a story will tell about a hero who goes o[n a] journey. Many different stories from around the world are about a hero's journey. In e[ach] story, the hero seems to follow the same pattern.

Usually, the story begins with the hero be[ing] sent on a journey. There is an important task t[hat] the hero must complete on this journey, but h[e is] not alone. The hero meets other characters w[ho] help him find his way and stay out of danger[. At] the end of the journey, the hero usually face[s a] villain and must pass a test. Once he passes [the] test, the hero is rewarded.

There are lots of stories that follow this sa[me] pattern. "Jack and the Beanstalk" is a g[ood] example. Jack goes on a journey up the stran[ge] beanstalk that grew from the magic beans. He gets help from a fairy and also from [the] giant's wife. At the end of the story, Jack must face the giant and cut down the beansta[lk.] Jack and his mother live happily ever after.

Movies sometimes follow this pattern. In "The Wizard of Oz," Dorothy goes on a jour[ney] to the land of Oz. She meets the scarecrow, the tin man, and the lion, who help her f[ind] her way to the wizard and stay out of danger. The wizard tests Dorothy by making [her] face the wicked witch. At the end of the story, Dorothy gets to return home.

It's interesting to compare different stories and see how they follow the same patt[ern] of events. The hero's journey can be found in fairy tales, folktales, myths, legends, a[nd] even movies. Of course, not all stories about heroes follow this same pattern. Her[oes] come in all shapes and sizes. Even so, knowing about the hero's journey is helpful. Wh[en] you read a story that follows the pattern, you can appreciate it even more.

Read each sentence and check whether it gives the main idea of the passage or a supporting detail.

	Main Idea	Supporting Detail
The hero is usually sent on a journey with a specific task.	✓	
"Jack and the Beanstalk" is an example of the hero's journey.		✓
Stories from around the world follow the pattern of the hero's journey.	✓	
The hero usually meets friends who help him on his journey.	✓	✓
Myths, folktales, legends, and even movies tell the story of the hero's journey.		✓
You can compare many different stories about heroes and find the same pattern of events.		✓
The scarecrow, lion, and tin man help Dorothy find her way to the wizard.		✓
At the end of the story, the hero must face the villain and pass a test.	✓	

Prince Sadaka

The African people have a folktale about a Swahili sultan and his son, Prince Sad[a]. The sultan had seven sons, and all but Sadaka had left home to travel the world. sultan missed his sons, but he was too old to go look for them himself. So Prince Sad[a] courageously set out on a journey to find his brothers.

Weeks passed as Sadaka sailed across the Indian Ocean. Sadaka was not g[ood] at reading maps, and he got lost many times. But he was adventurous and kind, so made many friends along the way.

Sadaka landed on an island and met some hungry birds. He gave them food, and birds helped Sadaka sort through his maps. On the next island, Sadaka fed barleycor[n] hungry crickets, and they shared their gossip. They had heard rumors about his broth[ers] and they directed Sadaka to the island of the djinns. The djinns were lonely spirits w[ho] frightened most people, but Prince Sadaka spent hours talking with them. In return, th[ey] told Sadaka that he could find his brothers on the island of Pemba. Sadaka knew that sultan of Pemba was a tricky man, so he would have to be careful.

The sultan of Pemba agreed to help Sadaka find his brothers if he could pass three s. For the first test, Sadaka had to sort three huge bags of seeds before sunrise. Iaka whistled out to his friends the birds. Just as they had helped him sort his maps, y helped him sort the seeds.

When the sultan came back in the morning, he was impressed that the seeds were sorted. He gave Sadaka his second test, which was to cut down a giant tree with one ke of his sword. This time, Sadaka asked the djinns for help. The djinns hollowed out tree, so Sadaka could easily cut it down with one stroke of his sword.

For the third test the sultan brought Sadaka to a ball at the palace. He told Sadaka to I his favorite daughter and dance with her. This time, Sadaka called on the chattering kets for help. The crickets whispered in Sadaka's ear and helped him find the sultan's orite daughter. As Sadaka danced with her, the sultan was very pleased.

The sultan told Sadaka what had happened to his brothers. When they came to nba, they had been very rude, so he put them into his dungeon. Because Sadaka ssed the three tests, the sultan let the brothers go free. And the sultan's daughter ught Sadaka was so clever, she agreed to marry him.

Decide if the sentence describes the story's setting, conflict, resolution, or theme. Connect each sentence with the correct word.

1. The story takes place in Africa and on the island of Pemba.

2. Prince Sadaka makes friends who help him find his way and pass the three tests.

3. If you are generous to those you meet, they will help you in your time of need.

4. Sadaka gets lost while searching for his brothers, and then he faces three difficult tests.

Setting

Conflict

Resolution

Theme

Summarize the plot of the story.

Prince Satacw
khah ta find
boners

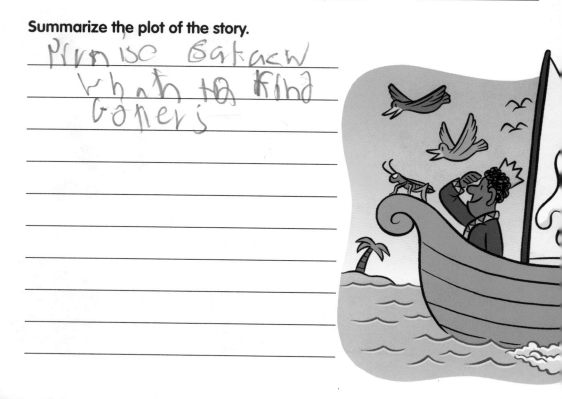

Answer the questions.

Why did Prince Sadaka go on a journey to find his brothers?

he did not see thin for a long time.

Why did Sadaka get lost as he sailed?

he is not good ato read maps

. What three friends did Sadaka make as he searched for his brothers?

bards caicts dijn,

. How did each friend help Sadaka find his brothers?

the tree tests

. What three tests did the sultan of Pemba give Sadaka?

sort fees cat tree, u ball an place it.

. How did Sadaka's friends help him pass the tests?

the baid sortsed dijh slash, catcksr staped

7. Why had the sultan of Pemba put the brothers in jail?

for being rooe,

8. Do you think Sadaka's story follows the pattern of the hero's journey?

yes

Colonial Careers

As you read the passage, look for the underlined sentences. If the statement is a fa[ct,] write an F in the box. If it's an opinion, write an O.

Colonial towns buzzed with activity from sunrise to sunset. There was always w[ork] to be done, and colonial people believed that laziness was a sin. Even children w[ere] expected to get up early and do chores. 1. **F** When a boy turned nine years old, [he] became an apprentice, or assistant. This is where he learned how to do one of the j[obs] in a colonial town. What were some of these job choices?

A cooper was important to the to[wn] because he worked with wood. A coo[per] fixed chairs, built barrels and tubs, and m[ade] wagon wheels. 2. **O** The miller, on the ot[her] hand, had a much more boring job. He [ran] the mill that ground grain for farmers. [The] farmers didn't pay the miller with mon[ey.] Instead, the miller kept a portion of the gr[ain] as payment.

3. **O** The blacksmith had the m[ost] interesting job in the town. The blacksm[ith] made things with iron, like horsesho[es,] pots, and nails. Farmers depended on blacksmiths to make hoes, plows, and ax[es.] Sometimes the blacksmith was a dentist because he had the right tools for pulling te[eth] out. 4. **F** Pulling people's teeth would be a terrible part of the job, especially duri[ng] colonial times.

The silversmith had a similar job as the blacksmith, but worked with silver instead [of] iron. 5. **F** Unlike most other colonial jobs, a woman could be a silversmith. A silversm[ith] made dinner dishes and silverware. Some people might buy plates from a pewter[er] instead of the silversmith. Pewter was more expensive than silver, so most colonis[ts] ld not afford it. 6.  <u>The pewterer's job was very important since only wealthy people could</u> <u>pewter.</u>

Colonial towns also had cobblers for making es. During this time the shoes were not cy. In fact, the cobbler used the same pattern every shoe, so the left and right shoes e exactly the same! 7. <u>Those shoes must e looked really strange.</u> While the cobblers de shoes, tailors and tanners made clothes. <u>The tailor used cloth and the tanner made hes from animal skins.</u> Tanners also made ther saddles and buckets. 9. <u>Working with ther seems very difficult, so being a tailor would a better job.</u>

Colonial kids had some interesting choices for eers. 10. <u>They usually worked as apprentices about seven years to learn their job.</u> Most onial people did the same job their whole life. ave them the chance to perfect their craft. The ter each person was at doing their job, the re useful they were to the town!

The Man with a Million Storie

Have you ever played the game "Marco Polo" in the pool? One swimmer clo his eyes and yells "Marco," and the other swimmers shout "Polo" in reply. With his e tightly shut, the swimmer explores the unknown water before him, following the sou of their voices. The game is named after a real explorer named Marco Polo, who o explored the unknown.

Born in Venice, Italy, Marco came from a family of traders and merchants. In fact, father and uncle had left on a journey before Marco was born, and they did not ret until he was fourteen years old! When the Polos left on their next trip, Marco went v them. The year was 1271, and Marco was 17 years old.

By 1275, the Polos reached China. They were welcomed by Kublai Khan, the lea of China at that time. Marco spent seventeen years exploring China and had m adventures. In 1295, the Polos finally returned to Venice. Marco was now 41 years o and he had been gone for 24 years. Marco loved telling stories about the incredi

things he had seen on his travels. The people of Ver called him *il milione* or *Marco milione*, for it was s that he had a million stories to tell.

Later, when Venice was at war with Genoa, Ma Polo was imprisoned. He passed the time in pris by telling stories about his adventures in China. Th was another prisoner who started writing down of Marco's stories. When they got out of prison, stories of Marco's travels were published. The bo inspired many other people to travel and explore. E Christopher Columbus had a copy of Marco Po stories when he sailed to America.

Many people did not believe Marco Polo when he talked about his journey. Th thought that he was making it all up. Even today, historians question his informatio They argue that Marco's descriptions of China were not accurate, so he must have eit made it up or been mistaken about where he was. But Marco Polo always defended tales. Before he died he said, "I didn't tell half of what I saw."

Find your way through the maze by connecting the events in the correct sequence.

START

Marco died arguing that "I did not tell half of what I saw."

Marco reached China and lived there for 17 years.

At 17, Marco left on a journey with his father and uncle.

When he returned to Venice, Marco told stories about his travels.

A book about Marco's travels was published.

People called Marco Polo "il millione."

Marco Polo was born in Venice, Italy.

Marco passed time in prison by telling stories of his adventures.

FINISH

To Buy or to Bring?

What did you have for lunch today? Did you bring your own lunch, or buy someth[...]
from the cafeteria? If you take a look around the lunch tables at Longmont Elementa[...]
you'll see both brown bags and cafeteria trays. We wanted to find out why some stude[...]
buy lunch and others bring it. So the Longmont Gazette conducted a poll. Here's w[...]
we found.

A little more than half of the students, 60%, said that they brought their own lu[...]
to school. Why do students choose to bring a packed lunch? The most popular reas[...]

en by 45% of the students, is that they did not like the cafeteria food. "The cafeteria
d does not taste good," said Ashley Jensen, "so I bring my lunch." Students who cited
 reason described cafeteria food as "bland" and "mushy."

Another 35% of the students said they bring a lunch because they have food allergies.
·y need to know exactly what they are eating, so they pack their own lunch. The final
% of the students bring their own lunch because it's faster. "I don't have to wait in the
, and I can start eating my lunch right away," fifth-grader Greg Johnston explained.
en Green agreed with Greg: "Bringing lunch means you can eat faster and have
re time to play."

Many students complain about cafeteria food, but 40% of Longmont students choose
buy food there. What are their reasons? A whopping 50% of the students said the
eteria gives you more choices. "If you bring your lunch from home you are limited,"
d Robin Olson. At the cafeteria you can buy hot food like pizza or a cold drink like milk.
stes better!" Katie Calvin pointed out that a sack lunch "sits in a bag all morning" but
eteria food tastes "fresh."

The next reason given by 40% of the students who buy lunch is that it's easier. As
drew Gibbons explains, "If I want to bring lunch, I have to pack it myself. Buying lunch
chool is easier, and the food is just as good." Many students said that it was easier
carry money to school to buy lunch than to carry a heavy lunch. Finally, 10% of the
dents buy lunch to be with their friends. "I'd rather buy lunch and hang out with my
nds in line than wait at the table for a long time," said Susan Madsen.

Whether you buy lunch or bring it, the important thing is to eat something healthy and
by your lunch break!

Use the information from the passage to label the percentages on the pie chart below.

It's faster
20%

Don't like cafeteria food.
45%

Allergies
35%

Be with friends
10%

It's easier
40%

More choices
50%

A **conclusion** is something that is not stated in the passage. You draw conclusions using clues from the text and your own logic.

1. Circle the most logical conclusion you can draw from the passage.
   a) Students who bring lunch are smarter than students who buy lunch.
   b) There are advantages and disadvantages to both buying and bringing lunch.
   c) The Longmont cafeteria needs to offer more food choices and have fresher food.

2. Read the conclusion and circle the clues that support it. There may be more than one correct clue!

   Conclusion: Buying food at the cafeteria might take a long time.

   Clues:
   a) Students with allergies prefer to bring lunch rather than buy at the cafeteria.
   b) Cafeteria food tastes fresher than food kept in a bag until lunch time.
   c) Students said they bring their lunch because it's faster than waiting in line.
   d) Susan Madsen said her friends take a long time to buy their lunches.

3. Find clues from the reading passage that support the conclusion. List the facts on the lines below.

   Conclusion: Students disagree about the taste of the cafeteria food.

   Clues: Ti taks bad
   if 6 %. say it taste
   bad   it is hos to
   hulshyc

   They thins it tastes
   bad and unhlithy, and
   45% fo pealpe thihl
   that.

Animal Astronauts

The first living thing to orbit Earth in a spaceship was not a human. It was a dog! dog's name was Laika, and the Soviet Union sent her into space in 1957. As Laika floate orbit, scientists monitored her heart rate, breathing, and blood pressure. They were abl learn about the effects of space travel on living things. Laika was only one of many anim who traveled in space, paving the way for human astronauts.

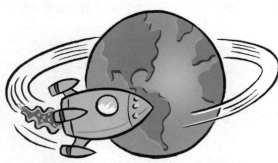

While the Soviets were sending d into space, the United States was send monkeys. In 1952, the United States sent t monkeys named Patricia and Mike into spc Scientists wanted to see what would happ when the spaceship accelerated to 2,0 miles per hour. As the spaceship flew to altitude of 36 miles, scientists watched the monkeys on a video signal. Thanks to Patri and Mike, they leaned that living things could survive the trip into space. Patricia c Mike landed safely and went to live at the National Zoological Park in Washington, D

Two more monkeys named Able and Baker were launched into space in 1959. T time, the spaceship went much higher and much faster. They flew 300 miles high c traveled over 10,000 miles per hour. After being weightless for nine minutes, Able c Baker returned to Earth in good condition. Their flight helped scientists learn even m about how space travel affects the body.

In 1961, the United States launched a chimp named Ham into space aboard a roc Ham had been trained to pull levers during the flight. This was an important step. Scienti learned that it was possible to perform tasks during a spaceflight. A few months af Ham's flight, the United States sent its first human astronaut, Alan Shepard, into spa The Soviet Union had already sent a man into space earlier that year. After more than t dogs had been launched into space, Yuri Gagarin was the first human to orbit Earth.

Animal astronauts helped pave the way for human astronauts. Thanks to the animals, scientists learned that humans could survive space travel.

Read each sentence and check whether it gives the main idea of the passage or a supporting detail.

	Main Idea	Supporting Detail
A dog named Laika was the first living thing to orbit Earth.	✓	
The United States sent monkeys named Patricia and Mike into space.	✓	
Many animals traveled into space and paved the way for human astronauts.		✓
Animal astronauts helped scientists learn how to send humans into space.		✓
Two monkeys named Able and Baker traveled 10,000 miles per hour in a spaceship.		✓
Animals helped scientists learn how space travel affects the body.	✓	
A chimp named Ham went into space and even pulled levers during flight.	✓	
Thanks to animals, scientists learned that humans could survive space travel.		✓

39

Teamwork

All the girls on the soccer team gathered around Coach Lund and waited for the [...] announcement.

"I think everyone will agree that Kelly will be a great team captain this year," Coa[...] Lund said. After the girls finished congratulating Kelly, Coach Lund handed her a sh[...] whistle she would use to help him run drills. She raced to the field to begin practi[...] smiling all the way.

As it turned out, helping the coach run practice drills was only one of Kell[...] responsibilities. Kelly also had to call all the girls on the team and remind them ab[...]

games. If the time or location changed, Kelly had to make sure everyone knew. anizing refreshments was also her responsibility. She filled the water jug and brought the field during practice. On game days a healthy snack needed to be provided for team. It seemed like there was no end to the details.

At the team's third game of the season, Kelly felt like a zombie on the field. Her mmate Julie passed her the ball, but Kelly wasn't paying attention. The other team got trol of the ball and made a goal.

"What happened out there?" Julie asked during the break. "I kicked the ball right to , and it was like you didn't even see it!"

"I'm sorry," Kelly said. "I had just realized that I forgot to remind everyone about the m photo. And I forgot to put cups by the water jug! I lost my focus." Kelly felt like crying. s wasn't the first time she had gotten distracted during a game. She was always rrying instead of concentrating on her playing. She even worried that maybe she just sn't a good enough leader to be the team captain.

"Playing your best and trying to win is more important than worrying about cups," e said. "My sister was team captain last year. She didn't try to do everything herself. other girls on the team helped out a lot. You just have to ask."

Kelly knew Julie was right. She looked for ways the team could support her. Since all girls on the team had e-mail, Julie agreed to send out reminders for the games over nail. Kelly also started a schedule to rotate who brought refreshments and cups. She had to follow up on things, but she saved a lot of time by sharing the workload.

Now that she was less overwhelmed, Kelly could return her attention to her game. e led her team all the way to the championship, and she even remembered to bring ps and refreshments to the final game.

Decide if the sentence describes the story's setting, conflict, resolution, or theme. Connect each sentence with the correct word.

1. Kelly asks her teammates to share some of the workload, and her playing improves.

2. A good leader works hard but also isn't afraid to let others help.

3. The story takes place at soccer practice and soccer games.

4. Kelly finds her duties as team captain overwhelming and she loses focus while playing.

Setting

Conflict

Resolution

Theme

This not rirc

Summarize the plot of the story.

Kelly asks her teammates to share some the workload, and her plainy improves

Answer the questions.

1. Why was Kelly smiling after Coach Lund gave her the whistle?

   She want to be the coach.

2. What were some of Kelly's responsibilities as team captain?

   She had to take care of everying

3. What did Julie confront Kelly about during the break?

   you are to hard on us

4. Why did Kelly lose focus while playing?

   She was to herd on them,

5. What advice did Julie give Kelly?

   ran and the cout with yous soccer ball

6. How did Kelly's teammates help share the workload?

   by playing

7. After Kelly asked for help, how did things change?

   beeves she is a kid

8. What qualities do you think make a good leader?

   brave, and rans,

A Letter from Philadelphia

As you read the passage, look for the underlined sentences.
If the statement is a fact, write an F in the box. If it's an opinion, write an O.

When I came to Philadelphia to visit Aunt Bon[ny] I had no idea what a great city this is! I've only be[en] here a few days, and already I've visited so m[any] wonderful places. 1.[O] Philadelphia is the best [city] on Earth!

One of our first stops was a tour of Independen[ce] Hall. 2.[F] This is where the Continental Congre[ss] met and signed the Declaration of Independen[ce] in 1776. It all happened in the Assembly Room. T[he] room looked small and simple, considering that fi[fty-] six men were all packed in there during the hott[est] months of the summer. 3.[F] Eleven years later, [the] United States Constitution was written in this v[ery] same building! 4.[O] It was really exciting to be i[n a] place with so much history.

We also went to see the Liberty Bell. Back [in] 1776, the bell rang to call people to Independen[ce] Square. 5.[F] It was there that the Declaration [of] Independence was first read aloud to the pub[lic.] The bell started to crack many years ago, but peop[le] preserved it. 6.[O] The line to see the Liberty Bell w[as] too long, but it was worth it!

The next day we went to visit Franklin Cou[rt.] This area is named after Benjamin Franklin, and [it] has all sorts of great things to see. I explored th[e]

underground museum and saw many of Franklin's inventions. 7.⟦D⟧ <u>The best part of the museum was an exhibit called the "Franklin Exchange."</u> In this exhibit, I could pick up a phone and call someone that corresponded with Franklin. Then I could listen to their exchange. What a great way to learn about this amazing man!

Since Ben Franklin was a printer, Franklin Court also has a print shop. I learned all about the history of printing. 8.⟦F⟧ <u>Ben Franklin also helped start the postal service.</u> At the museum about the history of the postal service, I saw mail ꭒches that were used on the Pony Express.

We also stopped at the Betsy Ross House. 9.⟦D⟧ <u>The story of Betsy Ross is very ɔiring.</u> She was a widow and she worked as a seamstress to support herself. She ꮩed the first American flag with white stars and red and white stripes. 10.⟦F⟧ <u>Congress ɔpted the flag on June 14, 1777, and this is why we celebrate Flag Day on that day.</u> Her ꭒse is decorated to look just as it would have back in the 1770s. Seeing furniture from ꮭ period was really interesting.

I am having such a great time, I want to come back again next summer. There is so ch to see and learn here, I'm sure I would never get bored. Seeing the places where ꭒortant historic events happened really makes history come alive!

A Bump in the Road

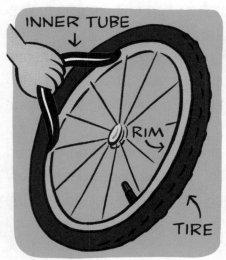

INNER TUBE

RIM

TIRE

You're riding your bike down a rocky lane, suddenly your front wheel wobbles out of contro small rock has pierced through the tire and mad hole. You've got a flat tire! Patching a hole in a b tire is easy if you follow these simple steps.

The first step is to let the rest of the air out of tire. Take off the valve cap and press down on valve. You can now remove the deflated tire from bike wheel. To do this, set the wheel on the fl Grab the metal rim and pry the tire away from it.

As you separate the tire from the rim, you'll a tube inside the tire. This is the "inner tube." You'll need to find where the hole is in inner tube. First, remove the inner tube from the tire. To find the hole, put the whole tu underwater. Look for where the bubbles are coming out, and that's where the hole is

Now it's time to patch the hole. Before you can put the patch on, the inner tu needs to be totally dry. Also, you need to roughen up the rubber on the inner tube. T will help the patch to stick better. Use sandpaper or a scraper, and rub the area arou the hole. Make sure there is no dirt on the fresh rubber. Spread some glue around hole, and then press the patch firmly on the tube. Let it dry for several minutes.

The tube is patched, and you can put your tire back together. Pump a little air back into the tube to give it a doughnut shape. Slide the inner tube back inside the tire. Then stretch the tire back over the metal rim. Your wheel is back to normal, and your bike is ready for another ride!

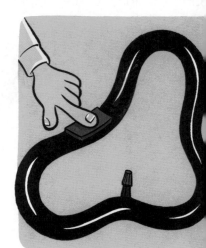

Find your way through the maze by connecting the events in the correct sequence.

ART

Let the glue dry for several minutes.

Pry the tire away from the rim and remove the inner tube.

Put the inner tube underwater to find the hole.

Let the remaining air out of the tire.

Use sandpaper to roughen up the rubber around the hole.

Spread glue on the tire and press the patch on.

Slide the tube back inside the tire and put the tire on the wheel.

Look for bubbles coming from the hole in the tube.

FINISH

Amazing Atoms

Have you ever wondered how many times you could divide something in half? L
say that you took an apple and cut it in half. Then you divided that half in two. Y
continued splitting each piece of the apple in half, over and over again. Would you e
get a piece that was so small it couldn't be divided?

As early as 400 BC a Greek thinker named Democritus asked this same questi
Democritus gazed at a long stretch of beach and realized that it was made of countle

ins of sand. Each grain of sand was tiny by itself, but millions of grains together formed each. He figured that all matter was made up of tiny, indestructable particles. He led these pieces *atomos,* which means "indivisible particle."

After Democritus died, it wasn't until the 1800s that scientists returned to his idea small, indivisible particles. Around 1803, a schoolteacher and chemist named John lton brought back the idea that atoms were the basic building blocks of all matter. He olained that different types of matter were made up of different types of atoms. The ms that make up a rock, for example, are different from the atoms that make up an ole. But all of the rock atoms are the same.

Another scientist built on this idea and started organizing the different atoms. Around 9, Dmitri Mendeleev started putting atoms into groups of elements based on atomic ight. He made a table to show all the different types of elements.

At this point, scientists knew that atoms existed and they knew how to weigh them. , they didn't know what the inside of an atom actually looked like. Around 1911, a entist named Ernest Rutherford figured out that there are tiny particles inside an atom. e very center of the atom is called the nucleus. Inside the nucleus there are small rticles with a positive charge called protons. Orbiting around the nucleus are particles th a negative charge called electrons. Later, scientists learned that the nucleus also ntained particles called neutrons, which have no charge.

Protons, neutrons, and electrons are very tiny and weigh very little. It would take billion electrons to weigh as much as a penny. It has taken scientists many years d lots of experiments to answer the question that Democritus first asked thousands years ago. As scientists continue to ask more questions, they discover even more out the atom!

Using the information from the passage, complete the diagram and the timeline below. Use the words in the box to label the diagram of the atom.

nucleus	proton	electron	orbit

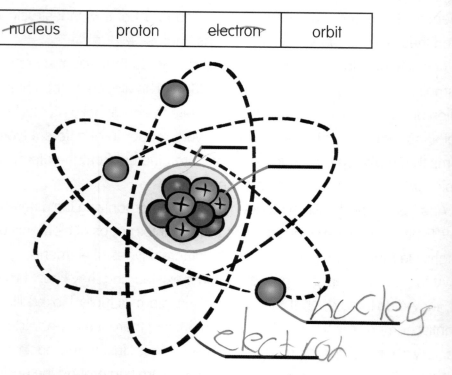

nucley

electron

Now fill in the blanks with words from the box to complete the timeline.

weight	inside	atomos	matter

400 BC   Democritus said that ___woight___ are tiny indestructible particles.

1803   John Dalton brought back the idea of atoms as basic building blocks of ___inside___.

1869   Dmitri Mendeleev organized atoms according to ___atomos___.

1911   Ernest Rutherford figured out what the ___matter___ of an atom looked like.

A **conclusion** is something that is not stated in the passage. You draw conclusions using clues from the text and your own logic.

1. Circle the most logical conclusion you can draw from the passage.
   a) As time passed, scientists got more and more confused about the atom.
   b) If scientists had worked harder, they would have discovered the atom earlier.
   c) Scientists built on each other's ideas to discover more about the atom.

2. Read the conclusion and circle the clues that support it. There may be more than one correct clue!
   Conclusion: At first, many people were not interested in the idea of the atom.
   Clues:
   a) After Democritus died, nobody studied the atom for over 2,000 years.
   b) Protons, neutrons, and electrons are tiny and do not weigh very much.
   c) It wasn't until 1803 that scientists starting thinking about the atom again.
   d) John Dalton was a schoolteacher and chemist.

3. Find clues from the reading passage that support the conclusion. List the facts on the lines below.
   Conclusion: The atom was not discovered by one person, but by many scientists over a long period of time.
   Clues: 1. becuse it was descved by Democtrs
   2. semesr stm wuher wat is
   nucleus,

51

Sequoyah

For many years, the people of the Cherokee t had no written language. They told stories to pass d their history, but they weren't able to record anythin Cherokee man named Sequoyah helped change By inventing a written language, Sequoyah helped Cherokee tribe preserve their culture.

Sequoyah had always been amazed by pe who made marks on paper to communicate, a pra the natives called "talking leaves." Sequoyah serve the War of 1812, and he watched the American sol writing orders and letters. As the soldiers recorded events of the war, Sequoyah realized that a writing system would help the Cher people record their own history. After the war, he dedicated his life to developing a wri Cherokee language.

It took twelve years for Sequoyah to complete the writing system. When he showed the alphabet to the chief leaders, they were upset. They believed that "tal leaves" were evil. Despite their reaction, Sequoyah's writing system spread quickly. language was officially adopted by the tribe in 1825. Within a few years, the Bible been translated into Cherokee along with many hymns. It only took about two we for someone who spoke Cherokee to learn Sequoyah's writing system. Thanks to alphabet, thousands of Cherokee people could read and write their own language.

Sequoyah's writing system had a huge impact on the Cherokee tribe. They could record their history and write letters and books. By 1828, the first Cherokee newsp was printed, making it the first Native American newspaper published in the Un States. Most importantly, the writing system allowed the tribe to create a written re of their culture. They could pass down their stories through storytelling and thro writing.

Today, there is a National Park in California named after Sequoyah. The giant tr in the park are called Sequoyah trees, and they remind us of how he brought "talk leaves" to the Cherokee tribe.

Read each sentence and check whether it gives the main idea of the passage or a supporting detail.

	Main Idea	Supporting Detail
By inventing a written language, Sequoyah helped his Cherokee tribe preserve their culture.		✓
Thanks to Sequoyah, thousands of Cherokee people could read and write their language.	✓	
During the War of 1812, Sequoyah watched American soldiers reading and writing.	✓	
It took twelve years for Sequoyah to develop his writing system.	✓	✓
Within a few years, the Bible had been translated into Cherokee along with many hymns.		
Sequoyah had a huge impact on the Cherokee tribe by creating a written Cherokee language.	✓	
By 1828, the first Cherokee newspaper was printed, making it the first Native American newspaper published in the United States.		✓
The Sequoyah trees of Sequoyah National Park are named after Sequoyah.	✓	

The Safe House

Leaves crunched under Martin's boots as he hiked through the woods in the darkn
He loved to walk through the woods that surrounded his family's plantation and loo
the stars. When Martin reached the edge of his family's property, he paused. The wor
who owned the house next door was hanging a lantern on the hitching post by her f
door. He had watched her hang this lantern the past few nights when he was out on
walks. Martin wondered why she would leave a lantern outside her house. The wor
lived alone and went to bed early. It didn't make sense.

As Martin sat down to tighten his boot laces, he heard rustling in the trees.
shadows emerged from the woods and approached the woman's house. When
reached the front door, the light of the lantern revealed that they were actually sla
They knocked on the door, and the woman quickly opened it and hustled them insid

Martin had heard that there was an underground network of people who hel
slaves escape to the free states or Canada. The slaves traveled by night and stoppe
"safe houses" to rest. The lantern on the hitching post must have been the signal that
woman's house was a "safe house." Those slaves in the house were runaways, and
was helping them escape!

If Martin told anyone about what he saw, the slaves would be severely punished, haps even killed. The woman would be punished as well. Martin felt very confused. had always felt that slavery was wrong and he understood why a slave would want be free. Should he let them get away with it?

Suddenly dogs barked and men shouted through the woods. It was the slave hunters, d they were probably looking for the runaways Martin had just seen. As the group closer, Martin saw the fierce look in the men's eyes and the dogs' sharp teeth. They emed so cold and cruel.

The men spotted Martin and called out to him. "We're after two runaways, just turned missing. Seen or heard anything out here, young man?"

Martin took a deep breath. "No," he said. "This is my family's plantation, and I walk se woods almost every night. Nothing unusual tonight."

"They must have gone the other way," the man said. He whistled to his dogs, and group ran off in the opposite direction. Martin breathed a sigh of relief. He felt good out what he had done. He decided he wouldn't tell anyone about the safe house. In own small way, he had helped a few slaves get a little closer to freedom.

Decide if the sentence describes the story's setting, conflict, resolution, or theme. Connect each sentence with the correct word.

1. Freedom is a right worth fighting and risking for.

2. When the slave hunters arrive, Martin decides not to turn in the runaways.

3. Martin wonders if he should turn in his neighbor and the runaway slaves.

4. The story takes place on a southern plantation before the Civil War.

Setting

Conflict

Resolution

Theme

Summarize the plot of the story.

srcle are
thay thgrun
sway,

Answer the questions.

1. What did Martin notice when he was out on his nightly walk?

   save thing to agan

2. Why did Martin find the woman's behavior strange?

   she lest them in,

3. How did Martin figure out that the woman was helping runaways?

   She is port of the Undergrad
   realroad.

4. What is a "safe house"?

   A placee for slave to cape,

5. What would have happened if Martin had turned in the woman and the runaways?

   sox wad gat arsad,

6. How do you think Martin felt when he saw the slave hunters?

   scared,

7. Why do you think Martin decided not to tell the slave hunters about the runaways?

   she would get then,

8. How did Martin feel after he told the slave hunters there was nothing unusual?

   Sarod to tell a lix,

The School Play

As you read the poster, look for the underlined sentences.
If the statement is a fact, write an F in the box.
If it's an opinion, write an O.

Play Auditions!
Wednesday, November 1
3:00 PM

1. **F** <u>Auditions for the school play will be held in the auditorium.</u> This year, we'll be putting on a play called "The First Thanksgiving." The play tells the story of the first Thanksgiving holiday. 2. **O** <u>You won't want to miss out on this chance to be a part of the show!</u> Students will play the parts of the pilgrims and the Native Americans. We also need students who can paint set backdrops, make props, and design costumes. 3. **O** <u>Working on sets and costumes is just as much fun as being in the play!</u>

Here are some guidelines:

- Students in grades 3–6 can audition.
- At the audition you will be asked to read some lines.
- 4. **O** <u>Auditioning is fun, so don't be afraid!</u>
- You must be available for rehearsals after school.
- Your parents must sign a permission slip for you to participate.
- 5. **F** <u>The play will be performed the day before Thanksgiving vacation.</u>

We hope to see everyone at the audition!

Eastshore Elementary School presents
"The First Thanksgiving"
3:30 PM, November 23

All students are invited to attend this year's school play, "The First Thanksgiving." 6. R̲ Students have been rehearsing after school all month long. You'll learn about American history as you watch the story unfold. It's important to support your friends who have worked so hard to put the show together. 7. O̲ Seeing the play is the best way to start your Thanksgiving vacation!

Tickets are free!
8. F̲ No food is allowed in the auditorium.
The play starts at 3:30, and no latecomers will be admitted.
9. O̲ Both young children and adults will enjoy it, so invite your families!
The play lasts for about an hour.
10. F̲ The refreshments served after the play will be delicious.

Using Your Imagination

To be a good reader, it is important to understand the role of setting, conflict, resolution, and theme in a story.
Use your imagination and fill in the lines below with details for your own story.

Setting: _____

_____

_____

_____

Conflict: _____

_____

_____

_____

Resolution: _____

_____

_____

_____

_____

Theme: _____

_____

_____

_____

_____